To Emma Juliet, Dorothy Snow, & all the Musketeers; let your imagination lead you.
Love,
Mama y Papa

THE FOURTH MUSKETEER

I can sing, I can dance, my name is Sir Lance!
I battled a dragon that invaded South France!
I'm a wizard, a knight; I'm the fourth Musketeer!
Call upon me and I will never show fear!
I'm as strong as a lion, and as fast as a deer,
I stand up the tallest when the enemy draws near!
Perhaps you have heard of the tales of I,
Believe it! It's true, I am able to fly!

But what is this?
What is this that I see?
The Dark Queen has come, she'll never take me!
Ready your weapons, and raise up your shields!!!!

No.....
No..........
No..............

I have fallen, the battle is done!

This is no joke, it's not even a prank,
I have been captured; now I must walk the plank!

What?
Is it over?

"Yes, you're done with your bath.
Now dry yourself and go do your homework!"

It is clear, what can I say,
Sir Lance lives to fight another day!

PABLO THE BULL

This is the story of Pablo the bull,
Pablo was orange and thought he was cool.
Pablo wore glasses, a scarf, and a hat.
Pablo was chubby, but some called him fat.

Pablo asked questions when nobody cared.
Pablo was different, they pointed and stared.

Pablo, he painted with canvas and oil.
Perspective and angles were Pablo's main joy.
Pablo was different, he set many trends.

Pablo was special, though nobody knew.
Pablo was a circle among many cubes.

Dad's Apple

An apple falls, but doesn't roll far.
I will always be there to open the jar.
To sit by your side and wish on a star.
An apple falls, but doesn't roll far.

Where Do Babies Come From

"Hey Zach, can I ask you a question?"
> "Sure, anything for my baby sister."
Where do babies come from?"
> "That, little Anne I do not know.
> Why don't you ask Mom, Dad, or Uncle Joe."

"Uncle Joe, where do babies come from?"
> "That, little Anne I cannot say.
> Why don't you ask your Mom, Dad, or your Aunt May."

"Aunt May, where do babies come from?"
> "That, little Anne I'm sure that I know, the problem you see is that I only know some.
> Why don't you ask your Dad or Mom."

"Dad, where do babies come from?"
> "Where do babies come from? That, little Anne is what you've asked me.
> I know, let's ask Mommy."

"Mommy, where do babies come from?"
> "That, little Anne is a fabulous question. I'm so happy, little Anne that you came to me.
> You see, babies come from mommies like me. They grow in our tummies and eat what we
> eat. They smile and cry and stretch out their feet. Then one day they're born and smile
> hello, but here is a secret that you do not know. There is a baby inside of me growing and
> such, she is your sister and loves you so much.

ASPECTS OF THE MOON

Looking at the sky,
The black night, the snow white moon,
Compassion and love.

THE MUSEUM OF ART

We went to the museum, the museum of art.
It was so big, so where should I start.

The garden was fine, as I waited in line.
I'm only a child, so I paid but a dime.

There were drawings, and paintings, and statues and such,
But the number one rule is that you should not touch.

You are welcome to talk, and encouraged to stare,
But do not go touching the man with stone hair.

There were paintings galore, what else could I say,
But then I saw something, it was a Monet.

It was blurry but clear, it was amazingly bright.
It was a church in mid daylight, a marvelous site.

How could he do this, a wizard with paint?
A magician on canvas, among artists a saint.

Did anyone see this? It was unique on its own.
This was so much better that a man carved of stone.

There was nothing better, nothing at all.
Not even the David that was 13ft tall.

I looked, and I looked, oh boy what a day!
I had just seen the art, the art of Monet.

Ballet Shoes

These shoes that dance and flutter around.
They pace back and forth to the rumbling sound.
That day has now come to make their appearance.
We've practiced and moved to the orchestras beat.
Now shoes become one as you dance on my feet.

Lucia

HOLA LUCIA

"Hola Maestra, yo soy Lucia."

"Why welcome Lucia, I am glad to see ya!"

"Vengo de lejos, me cuesta entender
Su idioma extraño que no se leer."

"Don't worry Lucia, we're all here to help.
We'll make your stay easy. I have no doubt.
You see, I was once a girl just like you,
Ven entra Lucia, we've been waiting for you."

Empty Pockets

Matt, he bought some of this and purchased some of that.
He bought a scarf, a sweater, and a big furry hat.
Matt bought a candy that was not at all small.
Matt bought so much, he bought nothing at all.

ROYGBIV

Red is for apples that make you feel good.
Orange for pumpkins that scare in the fall.
Yellow bananas that make you slip and then fall.
Green is moss that grows on wet trees.
Blue is for flowers that feed all the bees.
Indigo is blue that's hard to see, but believe me, it's pretty like the hues of the sea.
Violet is purple with blue at its heart, maybe a grape or delicious sweet tart.
These are the colors a rainbow displays, they help us recover from cold rainy days.

Dear Frida

Dear Frida,

You are beautiful and strong like an ocean swell.
I hope this letter finds you well.

You are strong and vibrant,
Like a radiant diamond.

The bird of paradise looks dull next to the shimmer of your hair,
Your eyes are wicked, I dare not stare.

You are full of life, I must paint your shadow,
You are a jungle, a monkey, a bird, a meadow.

I paint the walls of every building,
But nothing compares to the love you are wielding.

Rest up my dear, for I am here,
You are my doe, I am your deer.

Together we will paint the world in red, green, and shades of white,
Together we shall take flight.

Vamos, mi amor,
Te quiero mucho.

Love,
Diego

SMART JUICE

I have a big test and don't know what to do.
I study, and study and things don't go
through.

My teacher Miss Weldon, she says I am
smart.
That I should believe this deep down in my
heart.

I tell her, "No misses, you see I am flawed.
For I study and study and remember nothing
at all."

She tells me she has the answer to this,
A quick little sip of the Smart Juice she's
mixed.

I go for the bait; I have nothing to lose.
Today I'll be smart thanks to the juice.

I drank the elixir, and it burned its way
down.
I felt a burning sensation and heard a
thunderous sound.

The elixir, it's working! It went straight to my
brain.
I feel dizzy, yet strong and I don't feel much
pain.

I walk in the next morning with this magic
inside.
This test it can run, but boy it can't hide!

I was done within minutes, not sure how I
did.
The elixir had worked, I was now a smart kid.

Eight weeks passed on by and to my
surprise,
My scores had come in, oh what a delight.

I ran to her classroom to see how I've done.
A perfect 600, oh my I have won!

I believe it's the juice, for what else could it
be?

She says, "Don't be silly, it's water you
drank.
It's hours of studying that you have to
thank."

CRAYON

COLOR

What is a color, if not bright?
What is a color to your sight?

A box of crayons, with many hues?
A circus tent of pinks and blues?

A flower bed of yellow-red,
A purple peacock with a blue-green head.

A color is soft, a color is gentle.
A color is green just like a lentil.

A color is this, a color is that.
A color is a farmer with a yellow straw hat.

Never the less, this I must say,
All of these colors they brighten our day.

EDO

Edo is my breath,
Your beauty is in my heart,
My one-hundred views.

Wicked Milena

We have dreaded this, oh dear!
It is finally here!
The Wicked Milena,
Soon will appear!

We pick up our backpacks,
We line up with fright!
Ten months? Oh believe it,
She will eat you alive!

We hear her steps coming,
Earth trembles below.
Too late to run now,
To sixth grade we go!

Thirty step in,
Only twenty return!
At least those are some
Of the stories we've heard!

We enter her classroom,
We all take our seats.
We thought it'd be dreary,
A cavern indeed.

As you stare all around,
You will notice one thing.
Her classroom seems cheerful,
No gray tones- Just Pink!

We all take our seats,
We stare in despair.
We expect her to yell,
Oh, Milena, we're scared!

She says, "Nice to meet you.
I've waited so long,
To greet all my students
And start our year off."

Her smile seems sweet,
Her stare, not a glare.
She seems honest and friendly,
Some might even say fair.

Her eyes are light brown,
Not red like they've said.
Her voice gentle and singsong.
Wears a pink bow on her head.

She smiles with radiance,
Her teeth white as snow.
The end to this story,
We feel you should know.

She was not a tyrant.
She did not scream once.
She showed us she loved us.
She became one of us.

Ten months we spent with her.
We laughed every day.
She wanted the best for us,
And we wanted to stay.